THE OFFICIAL **NATIONAL PARK GUIDE**

NORTHUMBERLAND

Text and photographs by Tony Hopkins

SERIES EDITOR ROLY SMITH

PEVENSEY GUIDES

The Pevensey Press is an imprint of
David & Charles

First published in the UK in 2002

Map artwork by Ethan Danielson
based on material supplied by the
Northumberland National Park
Authority

A catalogue record for this book is
available from the British Library.

ISBN 1 898630 18 6 (paperback)

Edited by Sue Viccars
Book design by Les Dominey Design
Company, Exeter
and Printed in China by
CT Printing Ltd.
for David & Charles
Brunel House Newton Abbot Devon

Contents

Front cover: (top) Winter snow at the head of the Harthope Valley, looking towards Cheviot; (below) A well-preserved section of Hadrian's Wall at Walltown Crags; (front flap) Harbottle, in Coquetdale
Back cover: Hareshaw Linn; the waterfall lies at the end of a footpath following the Hareshaw Burn through attractive woodland near Bellingham
Page 1: Gorse (whin) blossom and andesite boulders, along the river Breamish near Bulby's Wood
Pages 2–3: Weathered and worn slabs of fell sandstone on the slopes of Simonside.
Left: Sheep-cropped terraces of bilberry and mat-grass on the slopes of West Hill, at the head of the College Valley

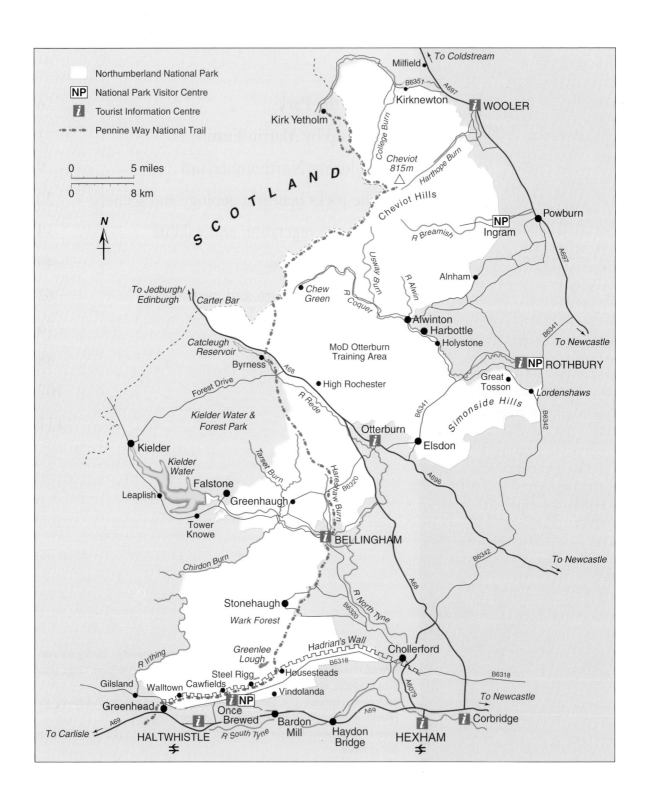

Northumberland National Park

NP   National Park Visitor Centre

i   Tourist Information Centre

Pennine Way National Trail

0   5 miles

0   8 km

N

Foreword

by Martin Fitton, Chief Executive, Association of National Park Authorities

The Northumberland National Park is one of our finest landscapes. Its location in the far north of England and its small population make it an area of great tranquillity. This belies its long history on the Border with Scotland, with all the drama that that has brought, perhaps made most clear by the evidence supplied by the remains of Hadrian's Wall.

Our National Parks are doubly special. Unlike many in the world, they are landscapes created, and largely maintained, by humans, mainly through farming. They are 'living landscapes' where change occurs through development in the villages and through changes in agricultural and forestry practices and the needs of the military. So when you visit the Park, remember that you are not simply looking at a beautiful landscape. You are seeing a place where people have lived and worked over many centuries.

National Parks are now cared for by independent planning authorities which hold land, provide grants to farmers and others; provide rangers, information, car parks and toilets; clear footpaths and litter, plant trees and partner many other agencies in pursuit of the purposes for which they exist. They are to conserve natural beauty, wildlife and cultural heritage and to promote the Parks' enjoyment by the public, while fostering the social and economic well-being of their residents.

Change has not always worked to the advantage of the National Parks. In Northumberland, for example, there has been a prolonged argument about the expansion of military training to include the use of large-tracked artillery. How this is resolved will, in the opinion of many, show how far we are prepared to protect these areas.

Natural beauty has also been affected by increased grazing encouraged by agricultural policies since World War II. obliging farmers to produce more in order to maintain an adequate standard of living. These policies are now changing, however, and the role farmers play in maintaining these beautiful landscapes is now recognised and funding is being provided to help them do this.

As a visitor, you can help sustain this wonderful landscape. Simply by being here, you are helping the local economy. You can help even more if you make a special effort to find and purchase local goods and services. This will mean that you become a more 'sustainable' tourist – a jargon word that expresses the challenging thought that we can look after the environment while enjoying the beauty of the countryside. You have probably arrived or intend to travel by car in the National Park. Once you get to the Park, consider leaving your car behind during at least part of your visit. You will enjoy the Park much more if you walk through its landscapes and stop and chat to those you meet, instead of trying to see everything in one visit.

In all of these ways, you can help protect the National Park while enjoying its beauty and tranquillity. It is a pleasure to welcome you.

Introducing Northumberland

An artist painting a view of the Northumberland hills would mix a palette of ochre, sienna and magenta, and sweep the brush across a broad canvas. Detail would be touched in later; scudding clouds, a rock face, a falcon. Years later, in a room far away, people might look at the picture and admire the falcon, the texture of the rocks and the brushwork in the sky. The painting would be about all of these things, but most of all it would be about a spirit in limitless space; the freedom to roam.

Every landscape has its own special qualities. Of all the National Parks, Northumberland is the most remote and least populated. Nowhere else in England can you see for miles and still be alone. However, the reason for the Park's apparent emptiness has less to do with its physical qualities than with its misfortune to have been caught time and again in the middle of other people's arguments.

The heyday of life in the Border hills probably came some time before the arrival of the Romans. While the quickening pace of change since then has smoothed out most other landscapes, the Border hills became a no-man's-land. Hadrian saw them as the haunt of barbarians, and built a wall to exclude them from his empire. After a burst of reflected glory as the Kingdom of Northumbria flared and faded, both William the Conqueror and Edward I marched armies to and fro and created a buffer zone between civilisation and the Scots. For the most formative centuries in rural history the Northumberland hills were a lawless waste. Instead of the southern idyll of pretty villages, hedgerows and coppices there were squat, grey bastles and windswept moors. Romantic poets did not tour the area with donkeys in search of majestic peaks and awesome cataracts. But when the army was looking for a place to practise trench warfare or give tanks their first taste of peatbogs, Winston Churchill knew just where to send them.

Curiously, this saga of misfortune has left behind a unique and valuable legacy. Because farming was such a perilous business, in a deteriorating climate and with a shrinking population, most of the uplands that had been ploughed and settled in prehistoric times were abandoned or used as rough grazing for

Pages 8–9
Top: The River North Tyne near Bellingham
Left: The Whin Sill at Walltown. In the foreground is a short section of Hadrian's Wall and the remains of Turret 44B. The nick in the whinstone ridge is a glacial meltwater channel

the best part of two millennia. Thus it is possible to wander over Garleigh Moor near Rothbury and stumble into the bracken-covered ramparts of an Iron Age hillfort, scramble across a cairnfield and bump into a sculpted Bronze Age boulder. Or sit on a Cheviot hillside and see, set out in shadows, an entire prehistoric landscape, the ghosts of field boundaries and hut circles.

Conservation by neglect, or by happy accident, is also the reason for the survival of wildlife habitats such as blanket bogs, mountain burns and alder thickets, places that owe nothing to human endeavour. These exist beside other primary habitats like scree slopes and cliff faces, and man-made or semi-natural habitats like prairie grasslands, hay meadows and forest plantations. The surviving mix, the presence of birds and animals that have been lost to most other parts of Britain, the effects of a frontier farming economy, the nearness of history and the exhilaration of having a wide open space all to yourself, is what makes the Northumberland National Park special.

The task of the National Park Authority and its partners is to stand up for the principles of landscape conservation – on which sustainable tourism depends – and so help to create a thriving community. Faced with having to access funds, resolve conflicting interests and balance arguments, even Solomon would have found it hard to make equitable judgements.

BOUNDARIES AND BORDERS

The boundary of Northumberland National Park was finalised in the early 1950s, after a decade of debates and discussions. Early suggestions by post-war enthusiasts had linked the Cheviots with the coast as one Park, and Hadrian's Wall and the North Pennines as another. The stumbling block was that the key landscapes, those that fulfilled the prerequisite of John Dower's ground-breaking report of 1945 by being areas of 'beautiful and relatively wild country', were linked by rich farmland. In the end a piecemeal compromise saw the creation of one National Park from the Wall to the Tweed, while the Northumberland Coast and the North Pennines became Areas of Outstanding Natural Beauty (AONBs). The differences in designation meant little to most people at the time, but landowners and their agents knew exactly where their best interests lay. Perhaps it would be a different story today; most farmers these days are grateful to be eligible for conservation grants.

Below: Whitsun Folk Gathering, at the Abbey Flags in Hexham
Opposite: Scattered oak/alder woodland on the slopes of Hare Law in the Cheviot Hills. In the foreground on the haughland of the College Burn are the remains of a circular stone sheep-stell

One of the well-worn statistics about Northumberland National Park is that in an area of 405sq miles (1,049sq km), the human population is less than 2,000. This certainly implies a wilderness, and Northumberland is one of England's quieter counties, almost a feudal back-water. The uplands of the Park are at least an hour's drive from the Metro Centre and other cultural icons of Tyneside. Even so, the size of the population is misleading and is another product of an artificial boundary. Several significant market towns, such as Hexham, Bellingham, Rothbury and Wooler, were excluded even though

Above: Early morning in Redesdale, north of West Woodburn. Many farms and settlements are protected from arctic winds by shelterbelts of sycamore trees

Pages 12–13: North from Garleigh Moor, towards Rothbury and Cragside

they are integral to the economic and social fabric of the area, and are all within a few minutes' cycle ride of the park. Thus it is impossible to get a true picture of life in the lonely uplands without walking around a bustling market square, listening to Northumbrian pipes or watching a Newcastle United football match in one of the village pubs, or visiting the marts and shepherds' shows that are the pivot of the farming year.

THE GREAT DIVIDE

The Park lies on a south-west/north-east axis, shadowing the cultural and physical divide of the Scottish border. Rain which falls on the Border can end up in the Irish Sea or the North Sea. In fact, some of the water gathered from the northern section of the Border Ridge starts by heading north-west into Scotland before looping east to go with the general flow. Three river systems serve the border headwaters, those of the Tyne, the Coquet and the Tweed. They and their tributary burns cut the uplands into distinct blocks or units.

FRONTIER LAND, AND THE WALL

The best, and least-known, part of the Park lies to the south, bounded by the Rivers Irthing and North Tyne. Cutting east–west parallel with the Tyne Gap lies the Whin Sill, a ridge of black dolerite, and along its switchback crest runs Hadrian's Wall. Together with its forts and the earlier Stanegate defences, it is the Wall which attracts most visitors to the region. They usually park off the Military Road, at Housesteads or Walltown or Cawfields, and climb from the patchwork of small farms and pastures onto the windswept crest. The Wall itself may then be a disappointment – in places it is missing altogether – but the sudden views of the big country to the north are a revelation. On a clear bright morning rolling pink prairie-grassland seems to drift as far as the eye can see, or to a smudged horizon of grey forest. Shallow lakes or loughs sparkle in the foreground, and the sound of wild geese, whooper swans or curlews carries for miles on the breeze and echoes around the crags.

Not many people walking the Wall take a detour through one of the ridge gaps and away from the steep scarp slope, or drive down one of the unfenced roads to the north that seem to lead to nowhere. If they did they would see the frontier from an outsider's perspective and discover what the barbarians knew; freedom is all in the mind, and the Romans were very good at mind games.

The great nothingness north of the Wall was the sort of place Tacitus had in mind when he reported what the British thought of Agricola and his army: 'They make a desolation, and call it peace'. Long after the Romans were forgotten this same sweep of country gained a reputation as bandit country, disputed land where reiving families preyed on each other and marcher lords tried to impose order out of chaos. Secret pathways, hidden graves and a handful of legends are all that are left.

Below: Elsdon pele tower in early summer

REIVING COUNTRY

The North Tyne provides a clear break in the spine of moorland. Hay meadows and pastures, woods and hedgerows of wych elm, ash and oak crowd the sides of the valley. The river is famous for its salmon, but is also a fastness for otter and goosander. The head of the Tyne lies beyond the Park boundary, in the Border Forest Park, and is impounded by Kielder Water. This man-made landscape has its own austere beauty, as well as organised watersports, cycling and angling. There are quiet, remote patches of moorland and mires around Kielderhead too, at least the equal of National Park moors and irresistible for those in search of primeval England.

Between Tynedale and Coquetdale stretches real Border country; Roman roads, outpost forts and marching camps, medieval bastle houses and pele towers, battlefields from the weary centuries of Anglo-Scottish conflict. The hills are sometimes flanked by matgrass, sometimes by heather. The landscape is spare and elemental rather than spectacular. The River Rede marks a clear division in the Park; Redesdale carries one of the busiest cross-border roads, via Carter Bar to Jedburgh. Nearby is the village of Elsdon, one of the most fascinating little settlements in England, and immediately to the east, rising steeply from the Grasslees Burn, is the distinctive outcrop of fell sandstone known as the Simonside Hills. This weathered plateau, flanked by forest and topped by grouse moors, has such a distinctive profile that it can be seen and recognised from Cumbria and County

Durham. The Simonsides were a favourite destination for Tynesiders too, long before National Parks were invented. Anyone growing up in the area would have known all about hidden caves, dwarfs and buried treasure. Recent research has shown there is substance behind some of the stories; the tors on Simonside's main ridge are actually massive piles of boulders covering prehistoric burial mounds, and all around the surrounding slopes there are cist burials, field boundaries, incised rock art and Iron Age hillforts. Plenty of work for the antiquary, and food for the imagination.

FIGHTING TALK

Beyond the Grasslees Valley and stretching from the Rede to Coquetdale, taking in some beautiful heather moorland and the grassland foothills of the Cheviots, is the Otterburn Training Area, a vast no-go area owned by the Ministry of Defence. For any walker with an empathy for the hills it seems wrong to find some of the best countryside ringed by red flags telling you to

Above: Fierce weather and treacherous peat hags on the slopes of The Cheviot, near the Hanging Stone at Scotsman's Knowe
Opposite: The Carey Burn, near Skirl Naked in the Harthope Valley

keep out. Not all the area is out of bounds, or closed all year, but it is still a daunting experience to find your quest for spiritual renewal interrupted by a notice telling you not to touch anything because it might explode and kill you. The conflict of national interests seems profound. However, it should be borne in mind that the army was here first, in 1911. Also, most people would accept that NATO needs trained forces and there are few extensive tracts of country available. Finally, and an inconvenient truth for those supporting open access, wildlife flourishes far better on military ranges than it does anywhere else.

To have a fifth of the Park off limits and another fifth buried under a blanket of spruce trees seems a waste of 'wilderness'. It certainly highlights the need for good working relationships between the Park Authority and its partners. The balance is a difficult one and the Authority has to be pragmatic rather than confrontational. National Park staff work with the MoD on grant schemes, habitat management plans and to get farms into Countryside Stewardship. In recent years the Authority has only once objected to a military development, which resulted in a Public Enquiry. Usually, Park purposes are best served by compromise.

THE WIDE BLUE YONDER

The Coquet is a gem of a river. It rises on the Border Ridge and cuts a quick-silver dash through a wide valley at the edge of the Cheviot massif. One of the best access routes into the high hills follows the river from farm to farm all the way up to the remote Roman marching camps at Chew Green. By following ancient drove roads north out of Coquetdale it is soon possible to be on the open hilltops, alone but for hundreds of pipits and skylarks, with faraway views and wrap-around skies. The walking, on springy turf and untrodden paths, is as good as it gets.

The Cheviots are a landscape unto themselves, a turbulent sea of moor and matgrass, overlying pink and grey volcanic lavas. Rivers radiate outwards from a granite core, centred on the 2,675ft (815m) whaleback summit of The Cheviot. However, the terrain on the highest ground, particularly along the Border Ridge linking the domed peaks of Mozie Law, Windy Gyle, Cairn Hill and The Schil, is peat-hags and heather rather than grass. Tom Stephenson, who first proposed the Pennine Way in 1935, always rated the Cheviots as his favourite walking country, but by following the Border Ridge all the way up from Coquethead to within spitting distance of Kirk Yetholm, this most famous of long-distance paths condemned tired walkers to a 20-mile (32km) morass at the end of their journey. Fortunately a lot of hard work by National Park volunteers has seen the worst sections flagged, so that intrepid souls can now enjoy the spectacular scenery of the Border Ridge without having to worry about sinking into it. For the rest of us, the best way to explore the far north of the National Park is to be guided by one of the little rivers or burns and let a footpath then lead you up and away, into the wide blue yonder.

Right: Bracken and heather clothe the flanks of Harbottle Moor. Birch and rowan trees cling to rock outcrops along the burnsides

1 The rocks beneath: geology and scenery

We live our lives in the blink of an eye, so it is hard to comprehend the immense periods of time over which landscapes have evolved over millions of years. As far as an understanding of geology is concerned we have the attention span of a gnat and the patience of Daffy Duck. But if seconds were centuries it would be a different matter. The world would be fourteen years old and we would wake each morning to the excitement of a new set of earthquakes and volcanoes, and new horizons to explore.

The story began for the Northumberland hills 400 million years ago in the Silurian Period; four seasons in our fourteen years. Thick ocean sediments were pushed together until they were scrunched up into mountains. The most dramatic British survivors of this apocalyptic event are now known as the Scottish Highlands, but there was some earth-folding closer to home too around the Borders. Thus the oldest geological outcrops in Northumberland National Park are in the stepped valley sides of the Rede and the Coquet; nothing dramatic, but a useful bottom line in geological history.

A few million years of apparent inactivity, during which any mountains were weathered down to a fraction of their original height, obscured the fact that the earth had not settled itself and was subject to ominous stresses and strains. Relief came in Devonian times with a resounding bang and a flurry of volcanoes, and from the mayhem of lava, ash and molten debris a new mountain massif was created; the Cheviot Hills. All this happened about 380 million years ago. What the area actually looked like when it was busy transforming itself is hard to imagine, but it must have been awesome, and deadly. When the volcanic vents finally plugged themselves and the dust cleared an area of over 350 square miles lay in pristine savagery. The mountains were huge. Great drifts of andesite, layer upon layer of 'extruded' lavas, stretched in all directions, topped here and there by smouldering mounds of rock fragments or pyroclasts, thrown up by the volcanic explosions. And as an afterthought, at the very core of the massif, molten rock was pushed up or 'intruded', cooled and solidified to create a fist of immutable granite.

CHEMISTRY OF THE HILLS

It is surprisingly easy to get a fleeting, but false, impression of the volcanic origins of the Cheviots by retreating a few miles, parking by the roadside at Edlingham or Callaly, or at the Border layby at Carter Bar, and looking to the wide expanse of domed hills which crowd the horizon. It is tempting to half close your eyes and imagine that the highest peaks, Hedgehope and The Cheviot, are sleeping volcanoes. They aren't. In fact most of the original vol-

Right: Big skies and big hills; the Cheviots from Barrow Law, looking towards Yarnspath Law and Kidland Forest

Left: February snows: a view across the Aln Valley, just outside the National Park, from Edlingham north-west over Thrunton Woods and Whittingham. The white-capped Cheviots complete the picture

Right: Rocks and boulders add colour and texture to the landscape. The top boulder, of bright andesite, is from the lower slopes of Humbleton Hill; the lower boulder, covered with moss and lichen, is from the upper, wetter slopes of Byrness Hill

canic material, hundreds if not thousands of feet of the top layers of andesite, have been eroded revealing the roof of what was the granitic heart of the hills. Where the actual volcanic cones were is impossible to tell; what remains as the highest ground, above the 2,000ft contour, is the more resistant intruded rock, the granite. But the impression of the Cheviots as a cluster of extinct volcanic cones is hard to resist. From afar there is an integrity and an aloofness that sets the place apart.

Close to, preferably underfoot, the Cheviots reveal a lot more about their chemistry. Andesite is a pretty rock, often a delicate pink-grey in colour, fine-grained but flecked with larger felspar crystals. It weathers into rounded boulders which line most streams or burns in the Cheviots. In a landscape with few cliff faces, the water-worn boulders are the best source for walling stone. Thus down the centuries farmers and itinerant Irish labourers have had to cart suitable material out of the valleys and far into the hills. How workers then managed to build drys-tone walls out of them is a marvel. Unlike sedimentary rocks such as sandstone or limestone, igneous rocks cannot be faced or split; a Cheviot wall is a demonstration of how to defy gravity, composed of round andesite boulders that look as if they could tumble down the hillside at the first breath of wind.

Sometimes when you are walking in the Cheviots you come across big andesite boulders ablaze with lichens, so that the ground colour of purple or salmon pink is almost hidden by splashes of calamine yellow, brick red and virid-ian; an alchemy of colours.

Soil weathered from andesite is relatively rich in plant nutrients. This, together with centuries of grazing, accounts for the dominance of grass on the hill slopes. But the broad hill crests and plateaux are boggy and characterised by drifts of cotton-grass and cloudberry; rain carries away any nutrients and leaves the ground sour and peaty. Where granite breaks cover on the tops of the highest hills the surface is even more acidic, the peat deep and the vegetation based around a coat of bog-moss. Although rainfall in the Cheviots is only half that of the Pennines, the effect on the Border Ridge is similar; a quagmire is created, and most people walking the Pennine Way take away mixed memories as a result.

Finding exposed granite is often quite difficult; the best place to look is along the burn sides, where grey or dirty-pink granite boulders turn up among the more abundant andesite. Granite is composed of the minerals quartz, felspar and mica and because it cooled slowly, deep underground, the crystals are large and very distinctive.

Curiously, one of the most important scenic elements in the Cheviot Hills is neither the normal andesite nor the granite, but the place where they meet. When molten magma was pushed up or intruded into the existing overlying andesite, it baked it and created a hardened meta-lava. After a few hundred million years of erosion the narrow band of baked andesite stands out in a ring or 'aureole,' picking out the edge of the granite in a wide arc of rocky tors. Stand at any vantage point with a view into the heart of the hills and the tors will be apparent, and they are priceless to photographers and discerning walkers. The Schil and Housey Crags and a host of other favourites would never feature in guidebooks without them.

Another geological postscript of volcanic upheavals was created by minor intrusions of magma through fissures in the andesite and granite, forming dykes and blobs or blisters of felsite and porphyrite in existing beds. One of these 'laccoliths' has long been exploited at Harden Quarry, near Biddlestone. The rock is known as Harden red or red whin, and for many decades it was used up and down the country as an attractive roadstone. It still graces The Mall in London, private drives and many motorway verges, but is no longer considered suitable for main road surfaces. The quarry is still working, and represents one of the few significant extractive industries in the National Park.

About 350 million years ago, the Old Red Sandstone or Devonian Period gave way to the Carboniferous, by which time the Cheviot volcano was little more than a stump or

Right: Heather moorland on the fell sandstone of Harbottle Crag, Coquetdale

Above: The College Valley, at the heart of the Cheviots, looking north-east over Mounthoolie and Fleehope towards the coast

Indeed, the geology that succeeded the Fell Sandstone is called the Scremerston Coal Group and the Lower Limestone Group.

However, in mid Northumberland things aren't so cut and dried. In the delta of the mighty river which deposited the mud and sand in the seas, a floristic hothouse developed, dominated by trees related to the mosses and ferns; in the waterlogged conditions, peat was laid down from the rotting vegetation, later to be covered by more mud and sand, then it stopped and the cycle of limestone, shale, sandstone and coal repeated many times to create Scremerston Coal Group. There was not a lot of limestone, and only some modest and localised coal seams, but they were enough to spark a clutch of drift mines in Redesdale and the upper North Tyne Valley.

The Carboniferous Era and the Limestone Group was less dramatic in Northumberland than in Yorkshire and Derbyshire, where immense deposits of hard limestone dominate the scenery. Our seas were too coastal here to yield much more than mud and sand. However, there must have been a few balmy millennia when the shallows were warm and calm enough to be awash with lime-secreting creatures. At a few places in the south of the National Park there are outcrops of impure limestone, sufficient to be of ecological value and to have provided raw material for a local lime industry in the eighteenth and nineteenth centuries. Farm kilns burnt limestone to produce slaked lime, suitable for mortar and to fertilise the 'sour' land.

Meanwhile, also in the eighteenth and nineteenth centuries but in another part of Northumberland, the Carboniferous strata was yielding coal, not just in dribs and drabs but in reliable veins and seams. Unimaginable wealth was around the corner, as of course was heartbreak and doom. But that is another story; none of this affected the hills and moors, save to make the area a spiritual release for those wage-slaves who could afford the bus fare.

The Carboniferous had one last trick up its sleeve. Right at the very end, less than 300 million years ago, there was another flurry of earthquakes and the whole Cheviot massif was pushed up and tilted. A series of faults appeared. These allowed strata to slip and rub together, creating channels along which rivers would later run. The spoke-like drainage pattern of Cheviot rivers, involving the College and Harthope burns and the Breamish and Coquet rivers, can be traced back almost literally to this event. Molten magma was then pushed up the cracks and creases in the earth's crust. Into the sandstone strata, squeezed like hot jam between layers of a sandwich cake, was laid a new ridge of igneous material, which cooled underground. Only later was it to be exposed by gradual erosion of the overlying rocks to create one of northern England's most famous landscape features, the Great Whin Sill.

WHINSTONE AND THE WALL

The molten or oozing rock which welled up to form the Whin Sill cooled very quickly; it was narrowly confined between old sediments and was therefore in contact with a lot of cold rock. As it contracted it took on a crystalline form, but unlike granite the crystals of this intrusive rock, called dolerite, had little time to develop and stayed small and close-packed.

Dolerite is instantly recognisable; dark grey, dense and impossible to split. Known locally as whinstone, the Romans could make no use of it for building the Wall except as rubble infill, but they valued its immutable presence. The gentle dip slope on the south side carried their roads and forts, while the north face is vertical, black, an unyielding deterrent.

Anyone walking the Wall today, following the route of the proposed National Trail, will not only notice how hard the dolerite outcrops feels

Below: Cawfields Quarry near Haltwhistle is managed as a picnic area by the National Park Authority. A good access point for reaching one of the best sections of Hadrian's Wall, the old quarry also provides a useful geological cross-section of the Whin Sill; the dolerite of the volcanic intrusion cooled quickly into hexagonal columns

THE WHIN SILL

Yard for yard the Whin Sill is probably the most influential rock outcrop in Britain. Some of the most cherished icons in the cultural landscape of the North are associated with it. It runs as a narrow dipping ridge; on the Northumberland coast it outcrops at Dunstanburgh and as the Farne Islands. It provides the promontaries on which Bamburgh and Dunstanburgh Castles stand. In County Durham it is responsible for High Forse and High Cup Nick, two features of unrivalled grandeur. In the middle, slicing across the foot of the National Park, it appears as a switchback rolling ridge, along which Hadrian's Wall was built. Nowhere is it especially high; it is simply in the right place and fits snugly into the scheme of things.

underfoot, even through the soles of heavy boots, but also that in several important places there are slices of the entire ridge missing. These were nibbled away by quarrying. At the turn of the twentieth century whinstone was in big demand, for road chippings, street sets and pavements. In most places the extinct quarry sites have weathered into the landscape so they are not much of an eyesore. At one site – the popular car park and picnic area at Cawfields – the little quarry left a neat cross-section of the ridge, making it easy to appreciate how the dolerite cooled into hexagonal columns (resembling the basalt cliffs of Staffa or the Giant's Causeway).

Nothing very dramatic happened to the National Park landscape for a very long time after the end of the Carboniferous period. Big events were rumbling on elsewhere, but in what would be northern England earth and fire declared a truce. The climate settled down, rivers cut their paths to the sea and forests flourished. However, although all the major landscape features were in place, there was a last twist as ice rather than fire made an impact.

These days we are all aware of the consequences of global warming and are told to expect hotter summers and milder winters. Two million years ago it was the opposite story; a chill crept over northern Europe and all the uplands were soon locked in ice. Whatever wildlife existed before the freeze-up, nothing survived. Ice sheets hundreds of metres thick covered even the highest ground. Under pressure, the ice sheets of northern England lurched very slowly eastwards then south, scouring any crags and old water-channels as they went.

FREEZE AND THAW

In fact there was not just one big freeze up in the Ice Ages but a series, interspersed with milder spells which saw vast amounts of debris – pebbles and boulders, mud and slurry – dumped as glaciers retreated, only to be scraped up again as a new cold snap arrived. Thus pebbles that must have originated in Dumfries can be found scattered along the Till, while bits of andesite from the Cheviots are picked up along the Yorkshire coast.

Apart from the obvious rounding off of the high hills and the broadening of Valleys, the Ice Ages imposed their own fine detail to the landscape. When the ice melted millions of gallons of water had to escape, and it often did this by creating new side-valleys or by cutting channels beneath the retreating ice sheets. Meltwater channels, cut through solid rock like a hot knife through butter, can be seen throughout the National Park – most spectacularly in the Whin Sill at such places as Sycamore Gap and in the Cheviots at Humbleton and Yeavering. And everywhere, pristine mineral-rich soils were heaped and spread about, as if to kick-start a Garden of Eden.

Time and again, tundra and marshland, then woodland spread north and west, but in the early days the woodland was composed of trees that are now extinct or are found only in exotic places like Japan and America. The most recent cold snap started about 26,000 years ago and was all over by 10,000 years ago. Not a long time, but sufficient to wipe the slate clean yet again. The pioneer arctic-alpine plants that colonised the fertile open uplands of Britain were soon isolated as the climate improved and birch/juniper woodland crept up the high valleys, followed by pine and eventually oak, alder and lime. One of the particular joys of Northumberland is to be able to stand on a hillside and understand how it all might have looked in those faraway days; patches of dwarf willow, downy birch and juniper grow within yards of where their ancestors set down roots in late or post-glacial times.

Above: Meltwater channel at Humbleton Hill near Wooler. On the skyline is the distinctive double-topped summit of Yeavering Bell Pages 32–3: Early summer over Holystone Common. Birch/juniper woodland flanks the marshy valley of Holystone Burn

2 Climate, vegetation and wildlife

Ancient Northumberland might be some people's idea of Eden before the Fall: a wilderness, inhabited by a few tribes of hunter-gatherers: a landscape of oak woodland, reed-lined lakes, mossy hillsides, cliffs and streams. All spoilt by our megalomaniac ancestors. If so, when did everything go wrong?

There are no witnesses to the loss of the Golden Age. But there are clues to a changing landscape everywhere, in the plant communities and the pollen record. What is obvious is that after the last Ice Age things moved quite quickly as the climate improved. In most of the uplands tundra gave way to heathland of dwarf birch, creeping willow and juniper, which were superseded by downy birch and pine. Cool dry summers turned warm and damp, and deciduous forest tracked across from the continent to clothe most of the lowlands.

By about 7,000 years ago northern England was enjoying its climatic optimum; the 'wildwood' then was a beautiful mix of oak, wych elm, alder, hazel, birch and pine. For a few thousand years things stayed much the same. Britain was an island by this time so any trees or associated wildlife that had not spread quickly enough were excluded. But, of course, our ancestors were a perfectly natural part of the system, following herds and harvesting fruits.

Perhaps when things really started to go wrong for the wildwood it was in Neolithic times, about 5,000 years ago. The climate changed, turning wetter. Nutrients were leached out of the soil, bogs developed and elm, which had been one of the commonest trees, suffered a rapid decline – probably through a form of Dutch elm disease. And farmers started to clear woodland to make way for arable crops and pasture. By the late Bronze Age and through the Iron Age significant areas of what is now the National Park were cleared and the soil soon declined in quality because of poor drainage and bad husbandry. Environmental damage is not something confined to twentieth-century agribusiness. There was also a further deterioration in the climate; acidic bogs started to develop where there had once been fields or forests.

By medieval times the pattern of the land was set. The Northumberland wildwood had been almost completely swept away from the lowlands and replaced by farmland – arable crops, hay meadows and inbye pasture. In the uplands only cleughs and denes (the steep meltwater channels of the foothills) had any woodland cover, and the open plateaux and hillsides had become extensive pasture, for sheep and cattle, grading into moorland and blanket bog.

However, one of the unique elements in the Northumberland countryside is that there was then a hiatus. There was no big investment, no widespread land improvement or agrarian progress at least until the late seventeenth

Right: The green fields of Coquetdale lie between the fell sandstone of Simonside and the distant volcanic massif of the Cheviots

century. Quite simply, the rural population was too busy trying to keep itself alive. Scottish wars and lawlessness had a direct impact on both rural society and what was possible on the land; anyone trying to invest or improve things made themselves sitting ducks for reivers. Farming was impoverished at a time when it was making giant strides elsewhere.

Only in the last century or so has the pattern of land use changed again, accelerating a decline in fertility through intensification and overstocking. Some artificial or man-made habitats have enhanced the landscape and biodiversity, of which grouse moorland is a shining example. Others have had the reverse effect, most notably the advent of coniferous afforestation. Altogether, what has happened to the Northumberland hills over the last few decades, even since the creation of the National Park in 1956, has resulted in an erosion of biodiversity and the special qualities we look for in protected landscapes.

Perhaps if we are looking for a Golden Age we really need to go no further back than the turn of the twentieth century, when the landscape was extensively farmed but not intensively exploited. The hay meadows of that era must have been a joy to behold, though unappreciated in their own time. With the advent of silage, artificial fertilisers and early cutting, the flower-rich meadows disappeared; only a pitiful handful remain, enough to be afforded almost individual attention. Four meadows in the National Park are Sites of Special Scientific Interest (SSSIs) and a few more are included in stewardship schemes.

Above: Damp grassy banks are sometimes turned mauve by the flowers of ragged robin (above) and melancholy thistle
Left: Snow often covers the heather of the high hills in late winter and early spring. When other roads have been clear for days those into the Cheviots are still treacherous. But if you can get safely to the valley heads the hills, the walking and the views are sensational

COLD COMFORT

Northumberland rejoices in the coldest climate in England. However, it is not a place of extremes; it suffers neither the Arctic weather of East Anglia nor the torrential downpours of the Pennines or the Lake District. Its weather is usually cool and breezy, and it has as much rain in summer as in winter. This influences both the natural vegetation of the hills and the demeanour of tourists.

The natural and semi-natural habitats found within the National Park reflect the long sequence of post-glacial changes and the influence of farming. Most of the landscape is grassland or moorland, but around the edges, in the

Above: Heather is usually at its best in late August. The patches around Darden Lough, north of Elsdon, are especially colourful

clefts and creases and in every out-of-the-way corner, there are examples of all the most fascinating biotypes.

Moorland is a very British landscape feature, covering vast areas of the uplands. People think of moors in terms of heather, but there are all sorts of moors. In Northumberland, most of the rolling hills are covered with grass; not juicy ryegrass but bent and fescue – rough pasture grasses able to cope with deteriorating soil quality, the staple diet of upland breeds of sheep and cattle. On higher ground, plateaux and hilltops in the Cheviots and across large areas north of Hadrian's Wall, other even less nutritious grasses dominate, notably mat-grass and purple moor-grass. These are the lowest common denominator in upland vegetation. If you treat a landscape badly enough for long enough you will end up with moor-grass. It says much for past poverty and insecurity in farming around the Borders that nowhere else in England will you see such vast monocultures of this vegetation.

Despite its culinary defects, purple moor-grass has its redeeming features. It is a pretty plant and creates pink oceans that swirl in the breeze and catch the silver and gold of sunlight. People associate *Molinia* prairies with the Wall country, where the views north seem to stretch forever. These days, these same views come up against conifer plantations on the far skyline, but it is still possible to imagine this as windswept reiving country – a limitless twilight world of whispering prairie. By contrast, mat-grass is more readily associated with the high hills. During the winter and spring the bleached swathes of stems and leaves have earned the Cheviot slopes the name 'white land'.

Most walks out of the Cheviot valleys will take you from improved 'inbye' fields around the valley farms – lambing and silage fields treated with artificial fertilisers – through wet pastures where hard rush has invaded the fescue, up dry ridges where bent grass dominates, onto slopes of bleached mat-grass and finally onto the tops, where moor-grass, cloudberry and heather make up the usual plant community. Heather is usually thought of as an acid-loving plant but in fact it is more a case of it disliking lime. Thus the andesite soils of the Cheviots, which are basic but low in calcium, are perfectly suitable, as are the whin soils of the Wall area. The reason heather has become scarce on many Cheviot hills is because of overgrazing. Only in recent years, with estates diversifying into grouse management and agencies like the Countryside Agency and the

Above: Managing grouse moors is a time-consuming business. Keepers burn strips of heather every few years creating a mosaic so that the grouse can find food and shelter in different parts of the moor

Below: Good management of the moors encourages other wildlife too. This young curlew hardly resembles its image in the National Park logo, but its beak will soon grow

National Park Authority offering stewardship support, has there been a significant increase in the dwarf scrub habitats dominated by heather. Critically, stock levels have been decreased and cattle and sheep are now inwintered (in large sheds) so the heather is no longer nibbled to oblivion.

The reason for the push to save heather moorland is that it is a rich and rare wildlife habitat. For generations we all took the sight of purple uplands for granted, not realising heather management was a tricky and time-consuming business, undertaken for a precise purpose – the management of grouse. When shooting grouse lost its cachet among estate owners sheep rearing became universal. In the Cheviots overstocking quickly led to grasses replacing heather. Elsewhere, particularly on the Fell Sandstone of Simonside and Harbottle, but also parts of Redesdale and the Wall country, heather has held its own and has

always been a strong visual element, the 'black land'.

Walking through flowering heather on a late-summer afternoon is a buzzing delight as bumblebees and hoverflies gather nectar and pollen. The heavy scent is indescribable. But Northumberland's heather moors have other seasonal highlights too, notably in spring when the bubbling song of curlews fills the air and adders come out to sunbathe on the path-sides. This is also the time for heavyweight day-flying moths to be on the wing; the emperor, northern eggar and fox-moth. A male moth's antennae can pick up the scent of an emerging female from half a mile away. To be harassed over by a fast-flying moth on an urgent romantic assignation is one of the lesser-known perils of the moors.

sheet of water abuts the National Park; the boundary was set before the valley was flooded so most of the dam wall is within the National Park. This technicality makes no difference to what people think about Kielder Water; they either love it or hate it.

Kielder Water can be breathtakingly beautiful. It can be a wonderful place to enjoy organised watersports, mountain biking and trout fishing. It looks like a slice of the Canadian outback: big forests and wide open water. But at the same time it is an austere place. The forests are plantations of alien spruce trees and the water is acidic and deep. And whereas Catcleugh can be a good place to see winter wildfowl, Kielder is usually wind-ruffled and bare. On the whole, such an entirely artificial landscape is probably best outside a National Park, whatever the scenic and leisure potential.

BURNS, RIVERS AND LINNS

English Nature rates the watercourses of Northumberland as the cleanest or least polluted in any of the National Parks. Some are crystal clear, others are peat-stained. Rain on the hills seeps through the peat into runnels and sikes, which form up into tumbling, noisy little burns, which are then gathered into attractive rivers like the Breamish and the Coquet. The gradient from source to sea is such that most of the Northumberland rivers are fast-flowing and stony. Only the North Tyne, which flows south-east from Kielder and gathers up peat-stained tributaries like the Tarset Burn and the Rede, has the length and breadth to change pace and moods.

Pick up a boulder from the icy shallows of any river, from the Breamish to the Irthing, and you will find its underside alive with the larvae of net-spinning caddis flies, mayflies and stoneflies. These insects are a staple food for birds

Left: Catcleugh Reservoir and Byrness village at the head of Redesdale
Below: Alder and gorse, on the banks of the River Breamish above Ingram

stands ⌐
Harthop
wonderf
that nati
windbre
The
Plan and
increase
doubled
through
ing sche

Ilderton Dodd and in the Breamish Valley. The irony is that none of this can be counted as conserving an important wildlife habitat because the original woodland vanished hundreds or thousands of years ago. Any new planting has to stand on its merits as a desirable enhancement or change of land use, something that may seem self-evident but is open to interpretation.

People these days are very critical of the old Forestry Commission, whose remit was to grow trees – any trees – at all costs. It remains a source of bewilderment that anyone could ever have believed it was in the national interest to plant millions of acres of alien conifers across the Northumberland hills. In postwar Britain anyone questioning the mass planting of Sitka spruce would probably have been accused of being unpatriotic. Times, and truths, change. A fifth of the National Park still lies swaddled under forest plantations, but over the coming years their composition and design will change. Whether any of this will help the fast-declining red squirrel in its last stronghold is a moot point.

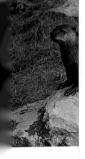

Above: Kidland Forest: an extensive spruce plantation high in the Cheviots. Sting Head, near Cushat Law
Opposite: Centuries old and going strong: alder trees on the banks of the Harthope Burn

3 Man's influence

Some places fire our imagination. When we look to a range of hills there is usually one peak that stands out, literally or in our mind's eye. What makes it special? Ten thousand years ago, when hunter-gatherers were tracking up the wooded plains and rivers into what are now the Northumberland hills, is there any reason to believe they didn't feel the same magic?

FAIRY STORIES AND SECRET SIGNS

From miles around, in any direction, Simonside draws the eye. The sandstone ridge, flanked by heather moorland and forest, broods over the Coquet Valley and the little town of Rothbury. Old shepherds tell stories of being lost there in sudden mists and of seeing shadowy figures. Simonside has a reputation for the worst sort of fairies, called duergars, who lure travellers to their deaths. There has always been something fey or pagan about the place.

And yet it is only in the last few years that archaeology has caught up with folk memory, to suggest that Simonside was a ritual landscape and perhaps even a sacred mountain. The clues are all around. The huge piles of stone that cap the high points of the ridge are prehistoric burial cairns. Bronze swords and flint arrowheads have been found wedged under sandstone boulders on the flanks of the hills. Beacon Hill must have been where bonfires were lit to signal the arrival of the Romans or the Angles – and in more recent times the French and the Scots. The forest hides dozens of early Bronze Age burial mounds, many with their cists or stone chambers lying open, their funerary urns removed by treasure-seekers or antiquaries.

Simonside is easy to explore but difficult to understand. Even the paths from the Forest Enterprise car park have stories to tell, or to hint at; several are hollow ways once used as drove routes to and from the Border, leading up and over the ridge, past enclosures and rock shelters where travellers once lit fires to ward off wolves and witches.

Above: Bronze Age burial chamber in a clearing of the forest plantation at Simonside
Left: Thropton, Coquetdale and the shadowy north face of the Simonside ridge

Less than a couple of miles from Simonside as the corbie flies, and within a stone's throw of a little car park on the B6342, is a low shoulder of heather moorland called Garleigh Moor or Lordenshaws. It is not as spectacular as the nearby sandstone ridge, but the landscape is just as magical. Every scatter of stones looks as if it has been placed for a purpose. Some hide burial mounds, others were piled up by Bronze Age farmers when they cleared the land for the plough. Perhaps the people who lived here and worked these slopes looked to Simonside as their local shrine – a place to be visited on special occasions, a place of spirits. Perhaps that is how the fairy stories started, passed like Chinese whispers from generation to generation, until the real meaning, the context, was lost.

Historic landscapes like Lordenshaws are hard to understand. Chronologies have big gaps; Stone Age hunter-gatherers and early farmers must have been here but they left nothing but a few flints. However, after the busy Bronze Age, the entire hill brow is enclosed within the ramparts of an Iron Age hillfort, dating from around 350BC. Hillforts were a sign of troubled times – the pastoral life of the uplands was far from idyllic. Then came the Roman period, by which time the ramparts had been taken out of use but a settlement of British roundhouses was established, which probably endured into the Dark Ages. Then came the Middle Ages, when this moorland was part of a deer park. Then – and this is the defining ingredient for visitors to Northumberland – then, nothing but sheep. If lead ore had been found here, or if farming had prospered as it did further away from the disputed Border, then this whole story of settlement would have been swept away. But there was a long spell of nothing and the imprint of lifestyles and cultures, one on another, has survived in the land.

GREEN HILLS AND LOST GLORIES

Aerial photographs of the northern half of the National Park, and especially the Cheviot foothills, are masterpieces of abstract shapes and texture. Neolithic henges are stamped in green circles, prehistoric field systems are picked out in cord-rigg on bracken banks with a stipple of clearance cairns; Romano-British settlements seem to huddle in the lee of almost every slope, and every other slope seems to be topped by a hillfort. Roman marching camps follow green roads, striking through prehistoric field systems and terraces. And over the top are cross-hatchings of medieval rigg and furrow ploughlands and the patchwork of eighteenth century enclosures. Apart from the aesthetic appeal of all this, an aerial view gives you the big picture; the land was worked for thousands of years while cultures came and went and settlements thrived and died.

Left: Garleigh Hill, close to Lordenshaws
Right: Cup and ring rock at Lordenshaws near Rothbury. In the background is the Simonside ridge, Beacon Hill and Dove Crag

ROCK ART

Glance at the OS map for the Lordenshaws area and tiny Gothic lettering springs out to spell 'cup and ring marked rocks'. These incised rocks appear in many places in the wilder parts of northern England, but they are rarely easy to find. At Lordenshaws you have a good chance of tripping over at least one. However, what you make of the enigmatic signs is another matter.

Were they art or astral maps? Did they have a spiritual significance? Nobody knows. But they were probably of ritual significance; they resemble the 'entoptic' geometric designs seen in the bushman art of southern Africa; designs created from trance images. They were probably etched into the rocks in Neolithic times, about 5,000 years ago. The main cup and ring rock at Lordenshaws is half-way up the hill slope, marked by an archaic Ministry of Works notice. The Horseshoe Rock is smaller, lower, and about 200yd (183m) to the north.

Above: Aerial view of the Iron Age hillfort at West Hill near Wooler in the Cheviot Hills (Tim Gates) Below: Ancient field systems crowd the hillsides above the Breamish Valley. In the centre of this aerial photograph is the excavation site at Turf Knowe (Tim Gates)

At ground level things are different; you can be standing in the middle of a historic landscape without seeing it. One of the National Park Authority's ongoing projects has been a series of archaeological digs in the hills above Ingram Farm in the Breamish Valley. The whole rolling hillscape is covered with humps and bumps, ridges and terraces. There are some very dramatic Iron Age hillforts (Brough Law, Middle Dene and Wether Hill) as well as Bronze Age cairns, hut circles, field boundaries, palisades and terraces. However, the purpose of the project is to find some clues and unravel the chronology, the patterns of prehistoric settlement and land use that are tucked away beneath the green pasture. Results so far are both revealing and tantalising: solving one mystery has often uncovered another.

The most tragic little story involves a place called Turf Knowe, a grassy knoll commanding a fine view of the Breamish and towards the distant coast. When excavated, the site was found to include two burial cairns. In one was a food vessel or pot and some cremated bones, dating back to 2,000 years BC. There were also the remains of a later cremation, and an iron spearhead. So this cairn had been built in the Bronze Age but re-used in the Dark Ages. The second cairn also contained food vessels and cremated bones, dated again to 2,000BC. But this time a careful study of some of the bone fragments revealed that they had belonged to an infant of about two years old, and that the infant had suffered from meningitis. Archaeology rarely tells such a heartbreaking or intimate story. It takes very little imagination to see a distraught family standing by the graveside at Turf Knowe, or to feel their grief.

Another of Northumberland's 'sacred mountains' lies at the northern edge of the Cheviots overlooking the Milfield Plain. This is Yeavering Bell, an impressive dome set apart from the other foothills beside the River Glen. It stands out, immutable and smooth-sided except for a drift of ancient elms and oaks around its feet. Its bald pate is broad and oval and is circled by a narrow crown of tumbled ramparts. An aerial view reveals the ghosts of 125 circular huts or houses within the ramparts. This hillfort is by far the biggest in the National Park and it must have been an important place when it was built about 2,500 years ago. Why people built hillforts is a mystery. Did they really feel so insecure, and who was going to attack them? Perhaps it was more like a statement of status by a chief or royal family. And why and when was it abandoned? The arrival of the Roman army must have changed the lives of privileged or powerful Iron Age dynasties, and put paid to the military potential of the forts, but the ordinary farming folk must simply have carried on as before; they had nowhere else to go.

As with Simonside and the Breamish Valley, there was more to Yeavering than its hillfort. It had already been part of a ritual landscape in Neolithic times and was aligned with henges or temples in the Milfield Plain. One of these henges stood at the foot of Yeavering, and nearby are the standing stones known as the Bendor Stone and the Battle Stone. Clearly, this place was magical, and it continued to weave a spell for thousands of years.

Above: Yeavering Bell from the B6351 near Kirknewton; close to the site of Ad Gefrin
Right: Ramparts encircle the twin peaks of Yeavering Bell, the biggest hillfort in the National Park
Opposite below: An exciting moment in the Turf Knowe excavations as a food vessel is lifted from a Bronze Age burial site. Later examination of the contents revealed bone fragments of an infant who had been suffering from meningitis (NNPA)

centuries. There are hundreds of them, usually within 20 miles (32km) of the border (an area defined in an act of 1555 as in need of special protection) and often within a stone's-throw of each other – possibly for added security. They are all built to the same blueprint; massively thick stone walls, tiny slit windows and shot holes, reinforced oak door, two storeys and a steeply pitched roof. In times of attack, the farmer and his family would have driven their bloodstock and stacked 'insight' (seed grain, tools, and so on) into the lower room and barred the door, climbed a ladder into the upper room, then closed the trapdoor and waited – sometimes for days, or until the reivers found a way of smoking them out.

Most existing bastle houses are in ruins or have been adapted or incorporated into barns and houses; spotting them is easy if you look for the huge boulders that were used for the footings. Perhaps the best group to see is that around Sidwood, at Black Middens (an English Heritage site) and Gatehouse (one bastle in ruins, the other on private land but easily viewed from the road). There is another picturesque group of bastles incoporated into Lowstead Farm, on the route of the Pennine Way, and the National Park Authority has recently completed consolidation and access work for sites at Low Cleughs near West Woodburn and Woodhouses near Harbottle. But while looking at bastle ruins and trying to imagine what it must have been like for sixteenth/seventeenth-century farmers, spare a thought for their labourers, who lived in turf-and-timber hovels and had nothing to lose but their lives.

Top: Lowstead, on the east bank of the Blacka Burn. The main farmhouse and byre are adapted from medieval bastle houses
Above: Windows were not a priority for bastle houses. Security and defence were what mattered. Note the big boulders and thick walls. Gatehouse, close to Tarset Burn
Opposite above: Woodhouses Bastle near Harbottle Grange. The original structure was adapted several times. Originally the roof would have been heather-thatched, but this was replaced by stone slates in 1904, when the house was still occupied. Extensive repair and consolidation was carried out by the National Park Authority in 1993
Opposite below: The bridleway heading west, below Humbleton Hill

MISERY AND MAGIC

It took centuries for the Border hills to recover from feuding and reiving; in many ways the landscape still reads as a testament to those years when the area was 'most wretched and miserable enough to burst the heart of a well-meaning pastor'. It was only in the eighteenth century that most ordinary farmhouses and steadings were built or rebuilt in stone, and even then the architecture echoed the bastle style; square and solid with no frills.

Drovers and shepherds walked the hills; the inbye fields were improved by the development of local lime kilns producing slaked lime to 'sweeten' the cold acid soil, but many of the old arable fields had already been turned into rough pasture. Northumberland was, and still is, a farming county and the hills reflect a strong pastoral tradition. There have been few alternative industries apart from small-scale coal mining and quarrying. Coke ovens and ironworks at Hareshaw failed within a few years of opening, leaving a few earthworks and a large dam, but no other significant industrial heritage.

History may well view the early twenty-first century as a time of travel and green tourism, with people feeling more in touch with the natural heritage than they have for centuries. Whether we can engage the same essential awe as a hunter-gatherer when confronted with virgin hills is open to question. However, we can certainly apply the perspective of having shared the landscape with a thousand more generations.

4 Land use, culture and customs

In most countries National Parks are wilderness areas, but busy little Britain is different. A visitor from America, Australia or Botswana would be astonished to see farmed, inhabited landscapes set aside as natural treasures. Farming plays an essential role in the conditions that define our version of National Parks; meadows and hedgerows, pastures and moors all exist in our Utopian vision of the countryside. When we close our eyes and think of England it is the landscape of Cobbet and Grigson that stretches before us.

Ten or twenty years ago no one would have predicted that the greatest threat to National Parks would be the meltdown of agriculture. All at once, hill farming is on a knife-edge as support mechanisms are being removed or replaced; change is inevitable. For Northumberland this means not just a risk to the fabric of the working environment but also to the mix of archaeology and ecology and to the cultural identity. Everything revolves around the way farming works.

Below: Winter feeding north of the Wall, at West Hotbank

Left: Roman noses are big in some sheep breeds. The blue-faced Leicester has a rather aristocratic nice-but-dim attitude

The pattern and character of the modern Border countryside was set in the seventeenth and eighteenth centuries; it was only with sustained peace that landowners looked to improving their income by enclosing land, seeding grasses and introducing new breeds of sheep. It is because of the earlier lack of security that medieval and prehistoric settlements and field systems survived, and it is because of the poverty of the population that there was little opposition to the enclosure of the commons when major landowners made a grab for the hills. Nobody regretted the passing of the cowboy days of reivers and drovers.

THE SHEEP'S IN THE MEADOWS, THE KYE'S IN THE CORN...

For the past two centuries sheep and suckler cows have been the mainstay of the Borders economy.

The sheep-farming year revolves around autumn marts, when farmers get a clear idea of what their labours are worth. Tups or rams are put out on the hills in November to mate with the ewes. In February the ewes are scanned to see if they are pregnant. Most carry single lambs; because of the harsh conditions those with twins are usually given additional feed. Hill sheep usually lamb in April or May, out on the open hills whatever the weather. If a farm has some better quality or improved pasture in the valley or close to the farmsteading the ewes may be lambed here on the inbye. Hill sheep are 'hefted' to a particular 'cut' of the hills; they will rarely stray far from their own familiar patch and know where to find shelter in bad conditions. Often, hill breeds will be crossed with lowland breeds to produce offspring with particular qualities such as a quick growth-rate or good mothering instinct. Thus the traditional way is to mate a blue-faced Leicester tup with a blackface ewe to produce a mule lamb, or a Border Leicester tup with a Cheviot ewe to produce a half-bred lamb. Until recently the lambs were then weaned and sold on to lowland

SPOTTING THE SHEEP BREEDS

Sheep breeds in the National Park derived from scrawny hill and heath varieties, culminating in the definitive Cheviot breed, suited to the foothills and valleys, and the blackface, at home on the moors and open hills. These two breeds can still be seen anywhere in the Northumberland uplands. The Cheviot is white-faced, hornless and has pricked ears, while the 'blackie' has a coal-black face, often with white mottling, and has horns. Swaledales have replaced or augmented blackface flocks in some places; they are longer-limbed, white-muzzled and (according to this writer at least) far less attractive.

Above: The cuddly-looking Galloway can be temperamental, especially when one of its blue-grey calves is near by

farms to be finished off, but the crash in market prices has forced many farmers to try a new strategy, bringing in Texel tups and fattening the lambs themselves.

Cattle ('kyes' in local dialect) were more important in the hills a century ago, when hardy breeds like the Galloway were outwintered and thousands of 'Irish' stirks or bullocks were bought in each year to be fattened on the outbye. These days continental breeds like Limousin and Simental reign supreme, and any calves are so sensitive to the weather that they have to be inwintered in vast sheds. Of course, these sheds influence the look of many upper valleys, but at least the stock is kept off the land in increasingly wet winters; this helps to conserve wildlife habitats and archaeological sites.

Valley fields are often cut for silage, which is the main source of winter fodder. Hay is now a rarity though by no means a thing of the past. Unfortunately the wildflowers that once graced the traditional hay meadows have vanished with the use of artificial fertilisers. Hay is made by cutting grass in midsummer and letting it dry before baling, whilst silage is cut early (allowing a second and third cut later in the season) and then gathered still damp into a clamp or baled in black plastic bags. These days virtually everything is wrapped, including 'haylage' – not quite hay but only partly-dry grass.

Most work done on farms today relies on a minimum of labour. Farmers, who are usually tenants, can rarely afford to employ anyone but their own family. Anything that requires special skill or equipment, such as silage-making and scanning, is contracted in. Clipping is no longer an annual opportunity to gather friends and neighbours for a hard day's work with a good social clipping supper afterwards. Instead, teams of Australians and New Zealanders arrive each summer, working their way up the valleys farm by farm. There is virtually no money in wool; managing sheep properly is often carried out at a loss.

Clearly, the whole philosophy of farming is changing. With the reform of the Common Agricultural Policy and the removal of annual premiums (the mainstay of farm incomes) farmers will have to look for new ways of managing their land. Directly or indirectly the role of the National Park Authority may be critical in this. Environmental payments, particularly through Countryside Stewardship schemes, are bound to increase. At present a third of farms within the Park are involved in Stewardship Schemes, and several million pounds a year is paid towards environmental projects. There are 230 farms in the National Park. Most of those in the south, around Hadrian's Wall and in Tynedale, are small and many are owner-occupied. In the north, in the Cheviots, there are a handful of landowners and just a few very extensive farms. In future there are likely to be more amalgamations to create bigger, more viable units. Diversification has seen some very odd industries arrive in the uplands, but it has also seen the welcome return of some traditional crafts and enterprises, such as cheesemaking and carpentry. In the Cheviots there has also been a big move to the management of grouse, enhancing heather moorland and vastly improving the ecological interest of the hills. Not all change is going to be for the worse, even for the farming community.

SHADOWLANDS

Superimposed on the farming pattern of the National Park are two other important 'industries' or land uses. They both have a big effect on the look of the land and its use by visitors. The first is afforestation and the second is the army. It could be argued that regiments of either spruce trees or gung-ho sappers are bad for the natural environment, but issues in National Parks are rarely so simple.

Most of the afforestation took place in and soon after the 1950s, when the Forestry Commission's remit was still to grow trees quickly, no matter what the environmental cost. The country was still haunted by the prospect of not having enough timber for pit props and aeroplanes in times of war, and any 'unproductive' land anywhere in Britain was fair game for purchase and planting. A Border Forest appeared almost overnight as the Commission bought dozens of farms to create state forests at Wark, Redesdale, Falstone, Rothbury, Harwood and Kidland. Special villages were built for forest workers, at Stonehaugh and Byrness, and over 3,500 acres of spruce trees were planted each year until the late 1960s.

Needless to say, this had a dramatic effect on both the landscape and the farming culture; after a brief and illusory lift from improved job prospects people witnessed the eerie sight of farms and homes falling derelict and drowning in a blue-green haze, then disappearing into silent shadows. Some

Above: Sheep work like dosing usually takes place in pens and sheds. This means flocks have to be shepherded to and fro, sometimes for miles at a time

unique archaeological sites and wildlife habitats also entered a twilight world from which they would never escape.

To compound the problem of inappropriate afforestation, government grants and incentives encouraged estates and syndicates to invest in private plantations, without any thought about public access or conservation, or how the timber would eventually be managed or extracted.

Forest Enterprise is the new agency (split off from the old monolith of the FC) responsible for managing Kielder, the Border Forest Park and the bulk of the plantations within the National Park. Their approach is more enlightened in that although they have to grow and sell timber, most of which is only suitable for chip-board and wood pulp, they recognise an environmental responsibility and are working with conservation agencies such as the National Park to improve both the appearance and biodiversity of conifer plantations. Most forests now have design plans, according to which only small blocks of trees will be felled at a time, and up to 10 per cent of any replanting will be of hardwoods (alder, ash, oak, hazel, and so on) following watercourses and natural features. And in some places the spruce blanket is being rolled back to reveal Bronze Age burial mounds, bastle-houses and bogs.

However, the bottom line is that half a per cent of the National Park is native woodland, compared with over 20 per cent alien conifer plantations. There is clearly a long way to go to get the conservation balance right.

An even more obvious conflict between 'access to the hills' and the 'national interest' is the presence of a substantial army range in the middle of the National Park. The Otterburn Training Area is the largest single live firing range in Britain and is used by NATO forces to practise infantry manoeuvres, artillery firing and air-to-ground attack. Thirty thousand soldiers a year use the ranges, which stretch from the Rede to the Coquet, from Chew Green and the Border Ridge down to Grasslees and Otterburn. A fifth of the Ministry of Defence land is of open access at all times; no live firing takes place and walking along footpaths is perfectly safe. The scenery is excellent too. However, for the other four-fifths access is impossible except for a few weeks in spring, or

SAD SONGS AND FORGOTTEN FARMS

In the expansion of afforestation in the 1950s, many hill farms were bought by the Forestry Commission and the land was planted with conifers. The farmhouses often fell derelict. These words are part of Rennie's Song; *the ballad was written on the wall of one such derelict farm in Wark Forest. Rennie Proudlock was a forest worker and belonged to a family of poets:*

> *What have they done tae the wild rolling hills?*
> *The sheep and the cattle are leaving the fells.*
> *The shepherd he walks with his gibbie and dog,*
> *And he treads the same path that his father once trod.*
>
> *Nae mair will they hear of his whistles and yells,*
> *As he gathers the lambs and the ewes to the stells,*
> *And the hills that slope gently way down to the streams,*
> *Will be silent and dark in their mantles of green.*
>
> *The hill farms are dying and the folk all but gone.*
> *Of Kate's House and Clintburn there's left scarce a stone,*
> *And The Green and Harelaw stand empty and decayed,*
> *Like cairns for a people and a life passed away.*

Opposite: Kidland Forest from Hogdon Law
Left: Ruined farm buildings at Shield on the Wall, on a frosty February morning

when firing is not taking place. Red danger flags fly when the Training Area is closed and notices warn of the risk of straying from the paths or touching anything along the way.

In recent years the Ministry of Defence has worked hard to support the local community and to encourage access wherever this is possible. However, for some people the issues are more visceral, more a matter of principal; the country needs an army which has to train somewhere, yet surely the wiring off of a fifth of the National Park contradicts its primary purpose.For the Park Authority the essential business is to reach an accommodation and to keep talking, Military training is in a state of almost constant flux; the present need for more mobile, longer range weapons may be reviewed in the light of political and world events. The landscape will endure.

Catcleugh, close to the Scottish Border at the head of Redesdale, was once the refuge of wild cats but now lends its name to the National Park's only substantial reservoir. Engineering schemes to supply water to thirsty cities have brought significant employment to rural areas over the years. Catcleugh was built in the 1900s and is linked to two intermediate reservoirs at Colt Crag and Whittle Dene, which in turn pipe water to Newcastle. It took a workforce of up to a thousand navvies to dig out Catcleugh and for the years they were employed on the site they and their families were housed in a 'tin town' of corrugated iron shacks. Because they came from all over Tyneside, with inherent rivalries and a risk of potential violence, families were split into two communities, called 'Newcastle' and 'Gateshead', on either bank of the River Rede. Whether this domestic separation prevented petty fights is doubtful; labouring work paid very well in those days, so drinking and gambling were popular recreational activity and the local police were kept busy.

NATURE INTO ART

Far from major conurbations and with such a tiny population, and with such a chequered history, it is hardly surprising that the Northumberland hills are an intellectual and cultural backwater. Capability Brown, doyen of landscape architects, was born within sight of the Cheviots, as were a clutch of clerics such as Ralph Erskine (1685–1752), who wrote such toe-tappers as 'Gospel

Above: Holystone village is used to living with the army
Right: Catcleugh Reservoir in Redesdale, about 4 (6.4km) miles from the Scottish border

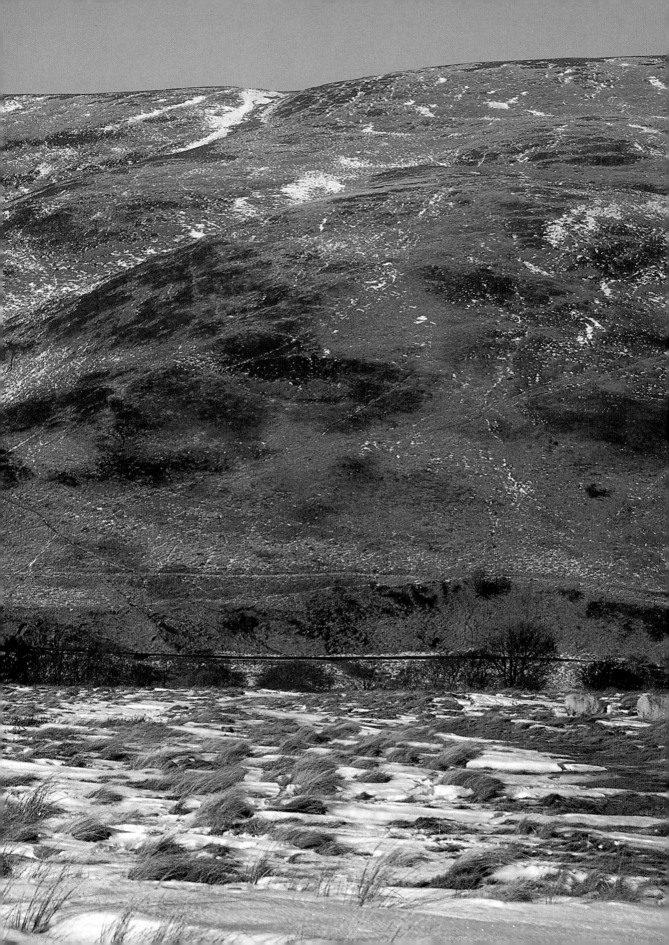

5 Recreation

Before the National Park was designated in 1956, the Northumberland hills were a popular place for Tynesiders to visit on summer Sundays. People toured in their Morris 1000s, parked in the haughland of the Breamish Valley, got out a picnic and read their Sunday paper. The same families now pull on their Goretex and take to the hills, or take their great grandchildren on an educational pond-dip. Attitudes and horizons change. The National Park Authority organises an imaginative programme of walks and events, but it can only scratch the surface of people's expanding interests.

For most visitors the Northumbrian hills hold two main attractions: wild walking and Roman ruins. The two can sometimes be combined but it is surprisingly difficult to imbue a big walk with a big theme. Thus the National Park has become an ideal place either for whole-day high hills walks or for short dips into classic countryside; last minute itineraries often based along Hadrian's Wall. Accessible car parks off the Military Road, at such places as Walltown Quarry, Cawfields, Steel Rigg and Housesteads, make it possible to link bracing stretches of the Whin Sill with visits to forts and prime sections of the Wall. The National Park Authority has a visitor centre at Once Brewed, there are excellent major Roman sites at Vindolanda, Housesteads and the Museum of the Roman Army at Carvoran, and there are several pubs within a few minutes drive. And for anyone without their own transport or who wants to see the key sites without being burdened by a drive, the National Park Authority runs a themed bus service between Carlisle and Hexham.

Away from Hadrian's Wall and Roman ruins, the archaeology of the National Park has long been under-appreciated – partly because of the lack of access and partly because there was a shortage of information about even the most dramatic sites. This has changed over the last few years and the Park

Above: Bringing history to life: the
Ermine Street Guard at Vindolanda
Below: Red flags fly when roads and
paths into the Otterburn Training
Area are closed
Opposite above: The Bendor Stone, a
Neolithic standing stone, near Akeld
at the north-east edge of the
National Park
Opposite below left: Thick walls and
a square view from Black Middens
bastle
Opposite below right: Millennium
Living History Project; the National
Park Authority working with children
at Low Cleughs Bastle
Pages 80–1: Stepping out in the
Cheviots, from Hindside Knowe to
Ward Law

Authority now produces several excellent leaflets describing short walks to such places as Yeavering Bell, Simonside and Humbleton Hill. Best of all, there is now a publication describing a hill-hopping route around the wonderful pre-historic landscape above the Breamish Valley, starting from the car park at Bulby's Wood. Taken together, and with major new projects in hand, the interpretation of the Park's archaeological heritage is perhaps the most exciting demonstration that the Park Authority is more than just a gathering of talking heads.

The renovation or consolidation of historic buildings as part of a recent 'Hidden Histories' initiative means that such places as Low Cleughs Bastle, Harbottle Castle and Tosson Tower are also accessible and interpreted; a great improvement on the days when people had to peer over 'no entry' signs and hope they were looking at the right pile of rubble. Again, there are many ways to enjoy the countryside and the advent of TV programmes like 'Time Team' have helped to create a new interest and awareness.

BIG COUNTRY, BIG WALKS

Walking is usually the means to an end, to achieve a view or experience a landscape in detail. But it is also an end in itself; people often set out for the hills for the pleasure of just walking in fresh air, over moss or turf. Most outdoor writers who know the northern half of Northumberland National Park rate it as the best walking country in England. The simple process of walking is itself a pleasure; the hills roll away into the far distance, the paths are springy underfoot and there are rarely any other people about. The weather may be unpredictable, but you can't have everything. The recent passing of the 'Right to Roam' Act will eventually provide even more opportunities for wild country walking.

Perhaps the finest walks are into the Cheviots, out of Coquetdale, northwards to the Border Ridge along forgotten drove roads like Clennel Street, from Alnham up the Salters' Road, or from Skirl Naked along the Harthope Valley, up to Housey Crag and onto Hedgehope. There are also excellent walks on the heather-clad sandstone ridges that arc around the Cheviots, from places like Hepple and out of the Grasslees Valley to Darden Lough.

One feature that sometimes puts people off several of the best big walks is that they run across Ministry of Defence land. As already mentioned, this highlights a conflict of national interests – the need to train an army with the National Park objective of access to outstanding countryside – but in practice there are few problems because a fifth of the Otterburn Training Area is designated for 'dry' training (ie no live firing) and is open to the public at all times. This fifth coincides with the classic walking country out of Harbottle and the Coquet Valley. Even the rest of the vast training area is not always off limits; access is possible for about eighty-five days a year along rights of way, when firing is not taking place. Red flags fly at every entrance to warn when the roads

ACTIVE SPORTS FOR ACTIVE SORTS

Fell racing or mixed events are organised annually for Cheviot and Simonside, but the sport is not as challenging here as it is in the Lake District or the Pennines. Similarly, the geology of the National Park is against pot-holing and hardly much more in favour of climbing. There are certainly some good and well-known climbing routes along the Whin Sill, at such places as Pele Crag, and on Fell Sandstone outcrops likes the Drake Stone.

Bouldering – practising moves for longer pitches elsewhere – is popular, and it is surprising how many outdoor centres find suitable abseiling sites in apparently unsuitable places. However, Northumberland is not a county of cliffs and crags and most Tyneside climbers head to the Lake District or the Highlands.

By contrast, several of the burns and rivers are suitable for canoeing; the North Tyne is a particular favourite, with flat and white-water sections, and is a great way to see wildlife like dippers and goosanders. The British Canoeing Union have a local access officer who can advise on gaining necessary permissions.

One of the more recent sports to take off in or around the National Park is

Opposite above: A welcome sight in the village of Falstone, close to Kielder Water
Opposite below: Lunchtime at the Salmon Inn, Holystone
Below: Fine weather and easy cycling along the Breamish Valley near Ingram

hang-gliding. Several of the domed Cheviot summits offer ideal launch sites, depending on thermal conditions and wind direction, and several local clubs organise meetings and offer advice on training. In a similar vein, gliding has become popular from Milfield aerodrome, close to the northern Cheviots; gliding must be an enviable way to gain an overview of the Beaumont Valley and the hillforts of Yeavering and Humbleton, but so far none of the Park Authority's archaeologists has dared to submit an appropriate travel claim.

BLAZING SADDLEBAGS

A system of bridleways, an open landscape and relatively few gates all add up to good prospects for horse-riding and off-road cycling. In fact although the National Park is a popular choice with horse-riders, the surface of the bridleway network is variable. This means that it is a good idea to check with the British Horse Society, which has a 'Code of Respect' and can advise through its local representative on suitable countryside. There is still some good terrain available in and around the National Park, and there are both organised and individual opportunities to saddle up and go on a day trek or a more challenging longer route.

Cycling can be a joy on quiet country roads; in fact Northumberland is one of the few places where road travel of any sort can still be a pleasure and people stop at cattle grids to say hello. Like horse-riding, cycling off-road relies on bridleways but there are several waymarked routes around the forests or on open hills. There is a Coquetdale Cycle Trail around the Rothbury area, a whole network of routes around Kielder, and a Hadrian's Wall cycle route which is due to open in 2003. Sustrans, the National Cycling Charity, is developing many waymarked long-distance routes that pass through or close by the National Park.

FISHING – AND FOOD

Coarse fishing is thin on the ground, but Northumberland has long had a reputation for its fly fishing along beautiful salmon rivers and trout streams. The North Tyne and the Coquet are especially popular, but in the National Park there are other good fishing opportunities.

A SIXTH BRIDGE FOR HARESHAW LINN

Each year the National Park hosts a number of events and activities for both visitors and residents. Recent funded projects have provided the Park Aurthority with the opportunity to work with local communities and schools on a number of heritage projects using oral history, developing community plays and creating living history events for schools.

The recent Hareshaw Linn project involved footpath and woodland work, but also the revival of Victorian traditions like the annual picnic and walk to the waterfall, poetry and rap writing by the local school and the production of a play by the Bellingham Drama Group. The creation of a special new bridge along the Hareshaw path close to the linn marks the culmination of the project.

Many clubs will sell day permits to visitors and these are usually available through local post offices or pubs. A day's fishing may not cost as much as might be expected – and sea trout are wonderful to watch, even if they are elusive to catch.

This leads us inexorably to food and eating. If you can't catch a sea trout or salmon, buy one at a place like Hexham or Alnwick, where the fishmongers usually sell wild-caught fish in the appropriate season. They may also sell local pheasant, rabbit and venison. Nearby you should be able to find a butcher selling superb local lamb, and a delicatessen stocking Redesdale cheese. After you have stocked up with these specialities stop off at a café for a cream tea, buy a local paper – the *Alnwick Advertiser* or the *Hexham Courant* – and see what events and activities have been organised for the week-end. Recreation comes in all shapes and sizes.

Above: *Conservation work in progress at Low Cleughs bastle (NNPA)*
Right: *Aerial view of Harbottle village. The ruins of the medieval castle are to the left (Tim Gates)*

6 Exploring the Park

ALNHAM

Alnham is one of the most interesting hamlets on the south-eastern edge of the Cheviot Hills, lying on an obvious nick point where ancient drove roads met and where a castle once protected the northern flank of Coquetdale. Little remains now, but there is a fine pele tower (privately owned) and an attractive little church, St Michael's, which has a compact graveyard and a pretty lych-gate. Although extensively restored in 1870 the nave and chancel are twelfth century. To the west of the church and pele tower and close to the site of the medieval village is a clear track leading north-west, out of the sheltering trees and onto the open hills. This is the Salter's Road, an ancient trackway from the coast to the border. It leads past some fine hills including Cushat Law, to the head of the Breamish Valley at Bleakhope, and to the border close to Uswayford. (NB Alnham is pronounced 'Yelnum', Bleakhope is 'Blaycup', and Uswayford is 'Oozyfud'. Cushat is the local name for a wood pigeon.)

ALWINTON

Upper Coquetdale can be a bleak and impressive place. The last village before you head into the heart of the Cheviots is Alwinton, a cluster of stone cottages around a village green and the little Hosedon Burn. Nearby is the Rose and Thistle pub and a National Park car park and toilet block. Back down the road is St Michael's Church, essentially Norman with nineteenth-century renovation. From the churchyard there are excellent views south over the narrowing Coquet Valley to heather-covered sandstone hills, whilst from the village northwards an ancient track called Clennel Street leads to the Border Ridge. Alwinton is the site of an annual Shepherds' Show, held the second Saturday in October.

BELLINGHAM

A large village, or small town, serving the North Tyne Valley and an important stop-over on the road to Kielder Water or for walkers on the Pennine Way. Bellingham can look dour if the sun isn't shining, but it has had to withstand so many Border raids that most of the older buildings have been burnt down several times. This was certainly the case with the thirteenth-century church, which has an unusual early seventeenth-century wagon-vaulted stone-slabbed roof. In the churchyard there is a gravestone shaped like an eighteenth-century pedlar's pack, the subject of a famous local legend involving a dastardly plan to rob a nearby hall. Someone called at the hall and left a 'long pack' to be collected later. A servant grew suspicious when he saw the pack move; he shot at it and killed a young robber hiding inside. That night the rest of the gang arrived expecting to be let into the house, but instead they were ambushed, overpowered and shot.

Bellingham (pronounced 'Bellinjum') has a variety of shops and pubs, a youth hostel and other facilities for walkers on the Pennine Way or for people visiting the National Park site at Hareshaw Linn. It also boasts a little market

Above: The curlew became the emblem of the National Park in 1957. The old oval design of the logo was replaced in the early 1990s

Above: Brisk business at Bellingham Mart

square, with a monument to soldiers of the Boer War, and nearby there is a mounted gun brought back from the Boxer rebellion in China. Bellingham has an interesting mart, bringing together farmers from north and south of the Border, and each year on the last Saturday in August the town plays host to a busy agricultural show.

BREAMISH VALLEY

A side road near Powburn on the A697 leads west through Ingram (see page 97) and beside the level ' haughland' of the pretty River Breamish for several miles into the heart of the Cheviots. The public road ends at Hartside but there is open access land along the way where cars can park, for picnics or from where to start a walk into the hills. The landscape is rich in archaeological remains, including the Iron Age hillfort at Brough Law and abundant prehistoric (Bronze Age and Romano-British) settlements. The best access for most of these is the car park at Bulby's Wood.

CAWFIELDS

Cawfields is an old whinstone quarry situated just north of the B6318 (Military Road), close to the (excellent) Milecastle Inn. The quarry site includes a deep dark pool, flowery banks and a picnic area, and is managed by the National Park Authority. The quarry took away a slice of the Whin Sill and Hadrian's Wall but this century-old vandalism has at least resulted in an unusual opportunity to see a cross section of the whin ridge, and to gain easy access to some of the best sections of the Wall. The vallum is very clearly defined across the

pastures to the east, and close by, visible from the side road to Shield on the Wall, are the Neolithic standing stones called the Mare and Foal.

CHEVIOT

Usually known as The Cheviot, this great whaleback of a hill lies at the centre of the Cheviot massif and is the highest point in Northumberland at 2,674ft (815m). Because it is composed of granite, The Cheviot's cap is covered in a mantle of waterlogged peat. The views aren't especially good either, compared with nearby Hedgehope. However, there is something special about being on the highest summit, and the dramatic ascent out of either the Harthope or the College Valleys usually makes the effort worthwhile.

CHEW GREEN

The ghost of Dere Street, the Roman Road from York to the barbarian wilderness of untamed Caledonia, crosses the Cheviots near the head of the River Coquet at a place called Chew Green. By driving from Alwinton as far as you can get westwards, past or through the isolated farms of Fulhope and Makendon, you arrive at a Ministry of Defence gate and a small car park. If a red flag is flying then further progress is impossible, but you can still get out of your car and explore the rough pasture to the north, uphill towards the Border, which is the site of an extensive Roman marching camp. Thousands of weary legionaries must have stopped here on their way to or from the farthest edge of the Empire. What is left looks like a few low grassy ridges and trenches, but in low sunlight the whole system leaps into relief. Chew Green is also an excellent place to park for a walk along the Border Ridge. And if the red flags are not flying and the MoD road is open you can drive on westwards into Redesdale.

COLLEGE VALLEY

The name is supposed to refer to a coven or college of witches who once practised in the area. The College is the least visited of all the Cheviot valleys; not only is it a long way from anywhere, at the northern edge of the National Park, but beyond Hethpool it is only accessible on foot or by private road. Cars are strictly limited and permits have to be obtained. All this means that the College Valley is a wonderful place to be; the flanking hills are elegant and the ancient alder trees along the College Burn are especially beautiful. At the foot of the valley is Hethpool Bell and the Collingwood Oaks – a gathering of half-grown oaks planted as acorns by Admiral Collingwood of Trafalgar fame. At the head of the valley beyond Mounthooly is the footpath up to Red Cribs, Hen Hole, and the spectacular Border Ridge.

*Opposite: The Mare and Foal standing stones, close to the Whin Sill near Shield on the Wall
Below: Hethpool Bell, and the Collingwood Oaks, from the Elsdon Burn*

ELSDON

Elsdon, gateway to Redesdale, is by far and away the most fascinating settlement within or close to the National Park boundary. The village is scattered around a wide green, used as a cattle pound in droving days as well as a venue for fairs and markets. It was also the site of a gallows and a pillory. At its upper northern side the green is dominated by St Cuthbert's Church and a pele tower. Both are of special interest. The church ('Cathedral of the Rede') is mainly fourteenth century but the narrow isles and transept indicate an older layout. Two stone coffin lids form the lintel of the entrance; one of them carries an engraved Celtic cross and a pair of shears. Inside the church there are inscribed stones including a Roman coffin, and close to the entrance the pillars carry grooves where swords were sharpened prior to battle. When the church was being built or extended in the late fourteenth century the foundations of the north wall were left shallow to avoid disturbing the remains of a mass grave – presumably the dead from the Battle of Otterburn.

Elsdon Pele is a classic fortified parsonage dating back to the Border Wars. Its walls are 3ft (1m) thick and its windows are small; a secure but austere and draughty dwelling. High on the south wall is a coat of arms, the shield of the Umfraville family, lords of Redesdale in Norman and medieval times. Across the Elsdon Burn are the grassy Mote Hills, site of the Umfraville's first castle and one of the best-preserved examples of a motte-and-bailey in Britain.

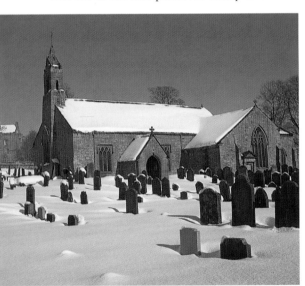

Left: St Cuthbert's Church, Elsdon
Below left: A pillar just inside the church door shows scratches and grooves thought to be where swords were sharpened during the Border Wars
Below: The Parson's pele at the north side of the green, Elsdon
Right: Elsdon from the east. The village is grouped around a wide green, dotted with trees. In the middle of the picture is the church, with the motte and bailey of a Norman castle on the far right

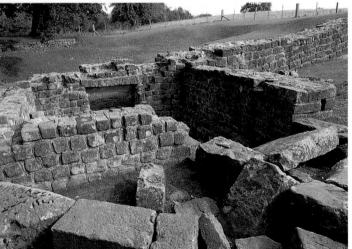

FALSTONE

This little village is now a stone's throw from Kielder Dam but it is a typical tree-bowered North Tyne settlement with a useful little shop. The churchyard has several interesting gravestones, including one depicting a little girl dancing with a skeleton.

GRASSLEES VALLEY

Native woodland, or woodland comprising native trees like oak and alder, is scarce as a significant landscape feature in the National Park. This makes the Grasslees, between Elsdon and Hepple, of special appeal. The area of the old Billsmoor deer park is especially attractive in the autumn when frosts have nipped the bracken and burnished the birches and oaks. The whole valley looks more like Sussex than Northumberland, though the distant views are clearly more attractive. Recently, fallow deer have been reintroduced at Billsmoor and they can sometimes be seen from the roadside, at the top of the hill as the road starts to descend northwards.

HADRIAN'S WALL

The Romans built nothing quite like the Wall anywhere north of the Sahara. It is one of the most famous ancient monuments in Europe, a World Heritage Site and the theme of the latest National Trail. Having said all that, most of the Wall is missing, and what remains is rarely more than 5 or 6ft (2m) high (and usually less). By far the most dramatic and most complete sections lie within the National Park, accessible from car parks off the Military Road, parallel with the A69 and served by the settlements of Haydon Bridge, Haltwhistle, Greenhead and Gilsland. There is much more to the Wall than just a wall; bridge abutments, forts and mileposts, bathhouses and aqueducts, defensive ditches and quarries, milecastles and civilian settlements all add to the fascination. Good starting points when visiting the area include the Once Brewed Visitor Centre and Housesteads Visitor Centre.

HALTWHISTLE

An unassuming little town on the banks of the South Tyne, outside the National Park but important because it provides accommodation and facilities and is close to the main east-west corridor of the A69. Haltwhistle also has a railway station and acts as a good starting point for anyone exploring the key central section of Hadrian's Wall.

HARBOTTLE

It is all too easy to miss Harbottle as you drive through it on your way up Coquetdale. It is a linear little village of grey-stone houses, pub and post office. One of the things that adds to the attraction of the place is the absence of over-head wires; an example of an early National Park conservation project to fund the undergrounding of unsightly cables. At the far side of the village and to the north, accessible from a small car park, is the grassy knoll and fragmented ruins of Harbottle Castle, the medieval base of the Umfraville family. A little further out of the village and to the south is a Forest Enterprise car park, giving access to heather moorland and the climb to the sandstone outcrop called the Drake Stone. There are excellent views from here north to the Cheviots. Nearby is an attractive little lake, the haunt of herons and dragonflies.

HARESHAW LINN

Owned by the National Park Authority and close to the route of the Pennine Way, the area known locally as The Linn comprises pastures, old iron work-ings and ancient woodland as well as a linn or waterfall. The beautiful oak/ash woodland on the flanks of the Hareshaw Burn is a scarce and valuable wildlife habitat – a perfect place to look and listen for wood warblers and redstarts. A path follows the burn upstream and across footbridges, leading to the pretti-est waterfall in Northumberland. There is a car park but the start of the walk is only a short distance from the middle of Bellingham.

HARTHOPE VALLEY

One of the main Cheviot valleys, leading from near Wooler via Happy Valley up to Langleeford. Road pull-offs allow you to park close to Langleeford and walk either south via Housey Crags onto Hedgehope or north via Scald Hill onto the Cheviot. Not the easiest ascent but guaranteed to be memorable.

Opposite above: Falstone from the old North British railway line
Opposite below: Bridge abutment near Chesters
Below: Hexham Abbey. Most of the present building of St Andrew's Church dates back to the late twelfth century

HEXHAM

Hexham is the main market town serving the Hadrian's Wall area and the southern third of the National Park. Although it has grown a little too big and busy over the past couple of decades Hexham is still a fascinating town with good medieval buildings and a fine abbey with famous Saxon crypt, Roman stones and St Wilfrid's 'throne', the Frith Stool. Good access to the west of the National Park.

HIGH ROCHESTER

For most of its journey through Northumberland, the busy A68 overlies or shad-ows the once-busy Roman

road called Dere Street. Being so far north of Hadrian's Wall, this stretch of Dere Street was half-way to the wilderness, a perfect place to station a cohort of soldiers to give prior warning of trouble further north and to keep the locals quiet. The Romans built one of their most important outpost forts, called Bremenium, here at High Rochester; the site lies along a track close to the war memorial at the south-east edge of the village. Further along the road at the far side of the village is Brigantium Archaeological Centre, a small 'reconstruction park' with a fine roundhouse, rock shelter, cup and ring marks and other characteristic features. It is possible to visit Brigantium and link this with a short walk along a waymarked path to Bremenium.

Above: The roundhouse reconstruction at Brigantium Archaeological Centre
Below: Lady's Well, a short walk from Holystone

HOLYSTONE

No more than a scatter of houses on the meandering banks of the Coquet, Holystone has a pleasant pub and a typical low, bell-turreted church. Footpaths from the hamlet lead west to an important local nature reserve, with fragments of juniper woodland and good heather moorland, and north to the tree-bowered pool called Lady's Well – or Holy Well. This is reputed to be an early-Christian baptism site associated with St Ninian. A stone cross stands in the centre of the pool with a statue, dedicated to St Paulinus, at the side.

HOUSESTEADS

This is certainly the most dramatically situated of all the forts along Hadrian's Wall. It is also the most popular and the busiest, so is best visited out of peak season if you want to enjoy the atmosphere of the place. Housesteads is perched on the crest of the Whin Sill and is integral with the Wall. The remains are extensive and clearly set out, so it is easy to get an idea of how the lay-out must have looked in the second century. Most people find the latrines (communal, with flush) the most fascinating feature. The views from the fort are excellent, and it is possible to walk east or west along the ridge for even better scenery. Housesteads is owned by the National Trust but most of the Wall is managed by English Heritage. The nearest access is from the National Park car park next to the National Trust Visitor Centre along the Military Road north of Bardon Mill. There is a steepish walk from the car park to the fort, which often catches out tourists in a hurry.

INGRAM

This is the only proper village of the Breamish Valley, situated on the banks of the river as it cuts into the Cheviots. Ingram lies at the edge of the National Park and the old schoolroom is now a National Park Visitor Centre, reached via a path from the bridge-end car park. Nearby is St Michael's Church, which suffered much at the hands of raiding Scots, who were adept at stripping lead from church roofs. The church is still solidly attractive, built on Norman foundations.

KIRKNEWTON

The scatter of hamlets along the northern edge of the Cheviots owe an allegiance to Scotland in terms of culture and vernacular architecture. Kirknewton is a typical example; its church contains a wonderful primitive relief sculpture showing the three Magi wearing kilts.

LORDENSHAWS

Close to the Simonside ridge and with extensive views north to the Cheviots and Cragside, the round crest of Lordenshaws on Garleigh Moor is at the heart of one of the most important prehistoric landscapes in the National Park. There are Bronze Age burials and field systems, rock art incised into sandstone blocks and an impressive Iron Age hillfort. The moorland is easy to explore for either a few minutes or a whole afternoon. It is also a good place for emperor moths and tiger beetles.

NORTH TYNE VALLEY

Most of Northumberland's river valleys are distinctly upland in character, with fast-flowing burns and rather steep rushy banks. The North Tyne is different; for much of its length it is broad and peaceful, indigo rather than peat-brown in

Top: The communal latrines; a popular feature of Housesteads Roman fort
Above: The National Park Visitor Centre in the old school room at Ingram
Below: Adoration of the (kilted) magi. St Gregory's Church, Kirknewton

Top: Percy's Cross near Otterburn. The pillar rests on the socket of the original Battle Stone, commemorating the Battle of Otterburn
Above: The Northumbrian cross at Rothbury
Pages 98–9: Willow, alder, wych elm, ash and hazel; the shady banks of the River North Tyne near Bellingham

colour, and it is the home of otters and salmon. The valley is broader too, with hay meadows (a rarity these days) and patches of woodland. This calmer atmosphere obscures the fact that the valley's history is as bloody as that of nearby Redesdale – the two communities were often involved in feuds and cattle rustling. The head of the North Tyne is now drowned in Kielder Water, which accounts for the controlled, regular flow of the river below the dam and down through Bellingham.

OTTERBURN

In Victorian times an 'Otterburn' was an essential travel item; a hard-wearing rug to keep you snug on a coach ride. Otterburn Mill was where these 'bull's lug' (ie heavy-duty) blankets or rugs were woven. The mill still stands but although it still has a shop (with associated café) it no longer weaves its own tweeds.

The village of Otterburn is one of the main settlements in Redesdale; the Ministry of Defence Training Area, Otterburn Hall and Otterburn Tower (now a hotel) lie close by. The latter was once the home of Mad Jack Hall, executed for his part in the Jacobite Rebellion of 1715. Sir Walter Scott also stayed here in 1812 whilst researching Border Ballads. To the west of the village and accessible along a pine-shaded footpath is Percy's Cross, commemorating the Battle of Otterburn in 1388.

REDESDALE

A distinct area of the National Park, associated with Border conflict and reiving families. The River Rede runs south-east from the Border at Carter Bar (once called Redeswire); the open valley is sometimes austere, often incredibly beautiful, as are its hamlets and villages. The main cross-border road, the A68, shadows Dere Street, the Roman road which links several important sites such as High Rochester and Chew Green.

ROTHBURY

Although outside the National Park, this is one of the most important bases for exploring the middle section of the National Park. The Simonside Hills lie close by, and Cragside Hall (one of the best-known National Trust properties in Northumberland) is just along the side road to the north, on the way to the A697 and the Cheviots. Rothbury is a pretty village built on a shoulder of the Coquet Valley, set along a steeply sloping tree-lined green with a tall Northumbrian cross at its heart.

All Saints Church is at least medieval in origin but restored or rebuilt in 1850. Inside the church the pedestal of the font is made up of a section of the original cross, a really wonderful example of stone-carving dating back to about 800 and containing relief images of vine-scroll animals and serpents devouring humans. Next to the church is a National Park Visitor Centre.

SIMONSIDE

A fell sandstone outcrop south-west of Rothbury, forming a dominant landscape feature made up a heather ridge flanked by conifer forest. A Forest Enterprise car park provides access through the woodland, up waymarked trails and past archaeological features such as Bronze Age burial cairns and a mysterious 'criss-cross' rock. The ridge walk, linking the main summit with Dove Crag and Beacon Hill, offers superb views and links with Lordenshaws, another important prehistoric landscape.

STONEHAUGH

When the Forestry Commission was fully engaged in creating a world of spruce it established several of its own villages to house the families of its workers and woodmen. Times changed and the anticipated workforce soon dwindled. Stonehaugh's thirty-five basic houses were built around 1957 and they look surreally out of place now, as do a set of full-size totem poles. The setting is fascinating; the Pennine Way runs close to the village to cross the Warks Burn, a pretty peaty stream in a green corridor through Warks Forest.

Below: Morning frost on the banks of the Warks Burn, Stonehaugh

VINDOLANDA

Although not on the line of Hadrian's Wall, Vindolanda is a key attraction for visitors. A Roman fort stood here at present-day Chesterholm as part of Agricola's Stanegate system. Rebuilt several times and incorporated as an essential part of the Hadrian's Wall defences, Vindolanda fort included an extensive civilian settlement. The remains have been excavated and have yielded impressive finds including hundreds of wooden writing tablets. The site is open to visitors and there are excellent reconstructions and a museum/visitor centre. Of all the places to visit along Hadrian's Wall this is the most interesting, with by far the best interpretation.

WALLTOWN

A side road off the Military Road east of Greenhead leads north to the line of Hadrian's Wall; to the left is the Museum of the Roman Army at Carvoran, and to the right is the extensive Walltown Quarry Recreation Site – an attractive area of grassland and a lake, on the site of the old whinstone quarry. This is a good starting point from which to explore the Wall; one of the most complete stretches lies to the east and there is now a clear route west along the Pennine Way to Thirlwall Castle.

WINTER'S GIBBET

This is an eerie, windswept spot on the Ottercops hills east of Elsdon, beside the Rothbury Road. A tall swinging gibbet, complete with a head (made of wood), marks the spot where the body of William Winter was hung in chains and left to rot, following his execution for murder in 1791. Beside the lay-by is a much older marker, the stone base of a medieval wooden cross.

WOOLER

The small town of Wooler is the gateway to the northern Cheviots, lying between the steeply rising hills and the Milfield Plain, on the banks of Wooler Water and close to its confluence with the Till. Wooler has shops and facilities, including a small visitor centre which provides information about the National Park and local features. There are good walks directly from the town, particularly to the west onto Coldberry and Humbleton Hills. Two or three miles to the south the Harthope Valley runs into the heart of the Cheviot massif for access to the high hills.

Opposite: Winter's Gibbet; a long-standing deterrent for anyone contemplating murder on the moors
Above: The water-filled stone socket of a medieval cross, close to Winter's Gibbet
Pages 104–5: Mallard enjoying the National Park recreation site at Walltown Quarry. The old whinstone quarry closed in the 1970s

Information

USEFUL ADDRESSES

Northumberland National Park
  Authority
Eastburn
South Park
Hexham
Northumberland NE46 1BS
Tel: 01434 605555

National Park Visitor Centres
Once Brewed Visitor Centre
Military Road
Bardon Mill
Northumberland NE65 7UP
Tel: 01434 344396/344777

Rothbury Visitor Centre
Church House
Church Street
Rothbury
Northumberland NE65 7UP
Tel: 01669 620887/620424

Ingram Visitor Centre
Powburn
Alnwick
Northumberland NE46 4LT
Tel: 01665 578248

Other Bodies
British Horse Society
National Agricultural Centre
Stoneleigh Park
Kenilworth
Warwickshire CV8 2XR
Tel: 01926 707700

Forestry Commission
Forest Enterprise
Kielder Forest District
Eals Burn
Bellingham
Northumberland NE48 2AJ
Tel: 01434 220242

The National Trust
Scots Gap
Morpeth
Northumberland NE61 4EG
Tel: 01670 774691

Northumberland Wildlife Trust
The Garden House
St Nicholas Park
Jubilee Road
Newcastle upon Tyne
NE43 3XT
Tel: 0191 284 6884

Northumbria Tourist Board
Aykley Heads
Durham DH1 5U
Tel: 0191 375 3000

The Range Liaison Officer
Ministry of Defence
Otterburn Training Area
Northumberland NE19 1NX
Tel: 0191 261 1046

Sustrans
Public Information Line
Tel: 0117 929 0888

Tower Knowe Visitor Centre
Kielder Water
Yarrow Moor
Hexham
Northumberland NE48 1BX
Tel: 01434 240398

Wooler Tourist Information
  Centre
Market Place
Wooler
Northumberland NE71 6LQ
Tel: 01668 282123

MAPS
The use of the appropriate
Ordnance Survey maps is highly
recommended for any detailed
exploration of the National
Park, especially if you are
venturing out into the
countryside.

Ordnance Survey Leisure Maps
(1:25,000 or 2in to the mile)
No 16 The Cheviot Hills
No 42 Kielder Water
No 43 Hadrian's Wall

Landranger (1:50,000, about 1in
to the mile)
No 75 Berwick-upon-Tweed
No 80 The Cheviot Hills
No 81 Alnwick and Rothbury
No 86 Haltwhistle
No 87 Hexham

*Opposite: The view west from
Nanny's Hill to Greenlee*

ATTRACTIONS

Chillingham Wild Cattle
  Association
Warden's Cottage
Chillingham
Northumberland NE66 5NP
Tel: 01668 215250

Chesters Roman Fort
Chollerford
Humshaugh
Northumberland NE 46 4EP
Tel: 01434 681379

Housesteads Roman Fort
Haydon Bridge
Northumberland NE47 6NN
Tel: 01434 344363

Vindolanda
Chesterholm Museum
Bardon Mill
Northumberland NE47 7JN
Tel: 01434 344277

Kielder Castle Forest Park
  Centre
Kielder Castle
Kielder
Northumberland NE 48 1ER
Tel: 01434 250209

Hancock Museum
Barras Bridge
Newcastle-upon-Tyne
NE2 4PT
Tel: 0191 222 6865

Museum of Antiquities
University of Newcastle-upon-
  Tyne
Newcastle-upon-Tyne
NE1 7RU
Tel: 0191 222 7849

Cragside House
Cragside
Rothbury
Northumberland
NE65 7PX
Tel: 01669 620333

Brigantium
High Rochester
Otterburn
Northumberland
Tel: 01830 520801

FURTHER READING

Beckensall, Stan. *British Prehistoric Rock Art* (Tempus, 1999)

Beckensall, Stan. *Northumberland: the Power of Place* (Tempus, 2001)

Breeze, D. and Dobson, B. *Hadrian's Wall* (Penguin, 1976)

Charlton, Beryl. *The Story of Redesdale* (Northumberland National Park, 1986)

Durham Keith and McBride, Angus. *The Border Reivers* (Osprey, 1995)

Hopkins, Tony. *The Cheviot Way of Life* (Northumberland National Park, 1995)

Hopkins, Tony. *Northumberland National Park* (Webb and Bower/Michael Joseph, 1987)

Hopkins, Tony. *Pennine Way North* (Aurum, 2000)

Johnson, Stephen. *Hadrian's Wall* (English Heritage, 1989)

MacDonald Fraser, George. *The Steel Bonnets* (Barrie and Jenkins/Pan, 1974)

Salter, Mike. *The Old Parish Churches of Northumberland* (Folly, 1997)

Tomlinson. *Comprehensive Guide to Northumberland* (Davis, 1985)

Various authors. *Northumbria Leisure Guide* (AA/OS, 1996)

Wright, Geoffrey. *The Northumbrian Uplands* (David & Charles, 1989)

Waddington, Clive. *Land of Legend* (CountryStore, 1999)

ACKNOWLEDGEMENTS

Thanks for advice and help from staff of the Northumberland National Park Authority. Thanks too to Brian Waters for a discussion on art; to Kathryn Tickell for background information about Northumbrian music, and to her father Mike for the words to *Rennie's Song*. Finally, thanks to my family, especially Andrew and Kaffie.

*Opposite: Spring sunshine and brandy-
coloured (ie peat-stained) water,
Holystone Burn
Page 110: Harbottle castle and village,
Coquetdale*

Index

Page numbers in *italics* indicate illustrations